SOUTH WEST
INDEPENDENT
GIN
GUIDE

Edition

1

Copyright © Salt Media Ltd

Published by Salt Media Ltd 2018

01271 859299

Email: ideas@saltmedia.co.uk

www.saltmedia.co.uk

Salt Media *Independent Gin Guide* team:
Zoe Appleton, Susy Atkins, Richard Bailey, Nick Cooper, Sophie Ellis, Kate Fenton, Kathryn Lewis, Abi Manning, Tamsin Powell, Jo Rees, Rosanna Rothery, Christopher Sheppard, Dale Stiling, Linda Weller and Selena Young.

Design and illustration: Salt Media

A big thank you to the *Independent Gin Guide* committee (meet them on page 134) for their expertise and enthusiasm, **headline sponsor** Luscombe Drinks **and sponsors** Dartington Crystal, Salcombe Distilling Co. and The Wrecking Coast Distillery.

Distilleries, bars, retailers and gin schools are invited to be included in the guide based on meeting strict and very high criteria, which, in the case of distilleries includes distilling the gin themselves in small batches, being independently owned and run, and providing a high quality gin experience. Bars and retailers are required to stock at least five of the gins eligible for entry in the guide and in the case of bars, provide a specific serve for each of these gins.

www.indygin.guide

@indyginguide

@indyginguide

CONTENTS

Welcome to the first edition of the *Independent Gin Guide*, a carefully curated collection of South West gins, plus the unmissable places to drink, buy and learn about them.

As gin lovers with an appreciation of true-craft spirits, we watched the British gin-volution with jubilation - until we couldn't hold back and had to jump in and create this guide.

We knew that, like us, you'd want to know where to find the real deal, those extraordinary sips which carry real provenance. That's why each of the gins, bars, schools and retailers included in the guide meet an extremely high quality criteria (read more on page 4). They're also all independently run in the South West of England, so the guide provides an authentic taste of the terroir.

Our sister publications, the *Trencherman's Guide* and *Independent Coffee Guides* have long inspired fans of fine dining and speciality coffee in their pursuit of the exceptional; we hope the *Independent Gin Guide* will do the same.

Huge thanks to everyone - from distillers to bartenders to gin lovers - who have helped us realise the vision.

Here's to some thrilling explorations of this new spirit of the age.

Jo Rees
Editor
Insider's Guide series

🐦 @indyginguide
📷 @indyginguide

SPIRIT
OF
REINVENTION

Drinks writer Susy Atkins loops the loop
on a rollercoaster ride through the highs
and lows of the history of gin

W e're living in the middle of the gin-naissance. No, that's not the first time this semi-pun has been used, but I can't help using such a brilliant word to capture the South West's premium gin scene.

A CULTURAL PHENOMENON

Gin-naissance not only references the splendid spirit itself, it also implies a cultural phenomenon, which is exactly what we have now as the world of mixers, cocktails, garnishes, gin bars and merchants expands and influences our idea of fine drinking.

It's hard to imagine, but only a few short years ago the gin scene was so different (and so boring). The generic G&T in a South West bar or hotel was usually the only big-brand option on optic, weakened with a warm saccharine mixer, and a limp slice of lemon plopped in. The late 20th century and Noughties were, no doubt, a dull time in gin's history.

HIGHS AND LOWS

Look further back, though, and our favourite spirit was always on a rollercoaster, from its initial rise in the 16th and 17th century (its origins in the Dutch herbal spirit jenever) to the low point of the Gin Craze in the early 18th century when poor quality and illicit gin created London's underworld of wastrels and drunks.

By Victorian times, new laws and much better spirit saw an upturn and resulted in many of the original gin palaces springing up. Then the cocktail scene of the early 20th century added another loop the loop before the spirit fell out of fashion again.

SEA CHANGE

Now we have this – our beautiful guide – testament to what one region of England alone can offer today in the way of fascinating artisan gins, myriad serving suggestions and inspiring hot-spots where you can buy and enjoy them.

So what's brought about this sea change? Firstly, don't underestimate the general trend for retro drinks, especially those with an obvious provenance. Well made gin from a local distillery, using regional botanicals, is every bit as popular as the products from the craft brewer, cider maker or the local farmers' market.

Then there's the search for complex flavours – many fine-spirit lovers have moved on from plain vodka and into the multilayered nuances of gin. And let's not overlook the beautifully designed modern gin bottles and labels which catch the eye of a collector.

In gin and tonic (originally, in the 19th century British colonies, tonic would have contained much more quinine to ward off malaria), we have the most favoured and easily prepped alcoholic mixed drink of them all. A good G&T is bliss, with only two key ingredients (save maybe a garnish or two) and ice.

Most of all, though, a long-fought change in the law in 2009 allowed the independent small-batch gin scene to flourish. Until then HMRC didn't grant licences to distillers making under 300 litres at a time. New London gin makers, Sipsmith, persuaded the government to change this, paving the way for many more small craft distilleries.

WELCOME TO
THE GIN-VOLUTION

The result of this change has been astonishing, particularly in the South West, where we are lucky enough to enjoy an exceptional bubble of premium gin. I reckon the can-do attitude of many artisanal entrepreneurs living in this region is one reason why the gin scene here is so vibrant; another

'Many fine-spirit lovers have moved into the multilayered nuances of gin'

Cafting cocktails at The Dark Horse
No. 71

is the inspiration drawn from the glorious landscape that surrounds us.

This might be expressed in a South West coastal gin, perhaps imbued with subtle sea salt and seaweed flavours, or the herbal waft of the wild plants clinging to the cliffs above. Or it might be a moorland gin, where the botanicals could include gorse, heather honey or juicy foraged wild berries.

EXQUISITE
ESSENCES

Botanicals? If you want to know gin, you do need to understand the wonderful ingredients that go into it. Gin is a spirit distilled or flavoured with fruits, leaves, seeds, bark, roots, spices and other natural ingredients. Juniper must be the dominant botanical and it's this member of the pine family that gives that distinctive bold, clean, almost resinous aroma and flavour.

Other traditional botanicals used the world over include coriander seeds, orris root and angelica, but beyond that, each distiller invents his or her own recipe – do look out for the wildly diverse botanicals used in the gins in this guide. Some, such as Sicilian orange or Provençal lavender, are more cosmopolitan, but their makers are firmly rooted in creating their spirit in the South West.

We are at the beginning of a new wave in spirits. Now that's worth raising a glass to.

'This member of the pine family gives that distinctive bold, almost resinous flavour'

Exceptionally independent

Exceptional gins deserve exceptional mixers. The new range of mixers from Luscombe Drinks in Devon goes way beyond the usual tonic - it opens up a world of creative possibilities.

G&T lover? You'll be spoilt for choice as the Luscombe range also includes cucumber, grapefruit, elderflower, Devon and Devon light tonic varieties to complement even the most unusual botanicals.

THE INSIDER'S GUIDE TO

Unsure whether to present gin in a highball or a copa, which ice works best in a G&T, or how to choose a garnish?

Susy Atkins serves up the low-down

SERVING

There's nothing wrong with a gin and tonic in a tumbler but better is a copa – a wide-bowled glass (rather like a large wine glass), with a long stem you can hold it by, rather than warming the drink with your hands. Copa glasses can take a lot of ice too.

TASTING

To sample a gin like a pro, pour a small measure (15ml) into a clean wine glass and swirl to release the aroma. Then sip a little bit neat, sloshing it around your mouth to get the most of the complex flavours. Then add twice as much tonic to the gin – or water if you prefer – and try it again to see how the gin tastes when 'cut'.

MIXERS

A fine gin deserves a fine tonic, so make sure you use a premium brand. If you prefer a lighter tonic with less sweetness for a drier G&T, you're in luck as there are several delicious ones around including Luscombe, Fever-Tree and Fentimans. Flavoured tonics, such as grapefruit or cucumber, can be delicious, but of course they add their own flavour to the gin, so choose your match carefully.

GARNISHES

These can be many and varied, but be aware that very strong flavours in a garnish might overpower the subtle nuances of a top-quality gin.

Garnishes don't have to be lemon or lime, either. Pink grapefruit is very much the garnish of the moment (check out how many gin brands have recommended it here) – as a wedge, slice or twist of zest. A slice of apple is popular too.

More unusual garnishes include bay or sage leaves, sprigs of thyme, mint, basil or tarragon, all sorts of fresh berries, thin sticks of young rhubarb, rock salt (go steady, just add a little), fresh ginger slices and a tiny piece of chilli.

Twist citrus fruit to release the juice and oils and bruise the garnish, or rub it on the edge of the glass to make it stronger.

CHILL

Chill anything you like – glasses, gin, tonic, cocktail ingredients. Use large ice cubes in a G&T, not small ones or (worse) ice chips or slush, which will dilute your drink very quickly.

FOOD MATCHING

It's a myth that gin doesn't go with food. Just try sipping neat cold gin or a G&T with salty-savoury snacks like olives, spreads and dips such as tapenade, aioli and anchoiade. It's also great with peppery salad leaves, and smoked, cured or ceviche fish and seafood.

STORING

Keep your opened gin bottles out of bright light and in a cool place. Even unopened bottles should be kept away from direct sources of heat.

'There's nothing wrong with a gin and tonic in a tumbler but better is a copa'

Start Point and Luscombe tonic in a Dartington stemless copa at
Salcombe Gin's Distillery Bar

HOW
TO
USE
THE
GUIDE

We've split the guide into sections to make your gin-ventures as clear as a crisp gin and tonic served over ice ...

TRUE-CRAFT GINS

Our collection of South West-distilled, artisan gins from independent alchemists.

GIN HAUNTS

Exceptional bars which serve premium small-batch gins with style.

GIN STORES

Where to stock your drinks cabinet with unusual and specialist gins.

GIN SCHOOLS

Develop your gin tasting and distilling skills.

MAPS & NUMBERS

Every gin, bar, store and school has a number so you can find them on the South West map on page 26 or in the index at the back of the book.

Don't forget to let us know how your South West gin journey unfolds. Share your pictures and finds with us at:

🐦 @indyginguide

📷 @indyginguide

INDYGIN.GUIDE

YOUR GIN ADVENTURES START HERE

GIN

Connoisseur's map of the South West

 True-Craft Gins

 Gin Haunts

 Gin Stores

 Gin Schools

Find the establishments in the guide
by looking for their number at the
top of the pages.

Locations are approximate

TRUE-CRAFT GINS

A collection of South West artisan gins
from independent alchemists

1 Cotswolds Dry Gin

Cotswolds is notable for its vibrant juicy citrus flavour and more gentle aromatic note of locally grown lavender.

It also has unusual hazy pearlescence when ice or tonic is added. This 'louche' comes from citrus oils and is due to the large quantity of fresh citrus peel used in the distilling process.

The gin was initially a small project at the Cotswolds Distillery, which was set up in 2014 to make whisky, but has been so popular that a larger second gin still was recently bought. This is a slow-distilled spirit made in a single shot in pot stills.

DISTILLERY
Cotswolds Distillery

ESTABLISHED
2014

GIN LAUNCHED
2014

LITRES PER YEAR
87,500

SISTER GIN
1616 Barrel
Aged Gin

DISTILLERY TOURS
Available

GINS SOLD
On site

Perfect pours

GIN AND TONIC

Serve with lots of ice and topped with Indian tonic water. Garnish with a slice of pink grapefruit and a fresh bay leaf.

WHITE NEGRONI

Mix gin with Lillet Blanc vermouth and Suze liqueur, and garnish with a twist of pink grapefruit peel.

www.cotswoldsdistillery.com   01608 238533

Phillip's Field, Whichford Road, Shipston-on-Stour, Warwickshire, CV36 5HG

Tasting notes

Beautifully fragrant with a subtle whiff of lavender, this bursts with citrus on the palate while still remaining, at heart, a classic London dry. Pearlescent swirls appear on addition of mixer or ice.

ABV 46%

2 Garden Swift

Barney Wilczak, who founded Cirencester's Capreolus Distillery in 2015, has a passion for eaux de vie. And in Garden Swift (named after the beautiful gold swift moth) he aimed to capture the complexity and finesse of the best eaux de vie – but in a gin.

After many trials, he settled on no less than 34 botanicals. The exact recipe is secret, but includes plenty of organic Sicilian blood orange zest (cut on site) and flowers of the small-leafed lime tree, *Tilia cordata*.

Garden Swift displays fascinating swirls of hazy pearlescence when chilled or mixed with tonic.

DISTILLERY
Capreolus Distillery

ESTABLISHED
2015

GIN LAUNCHED
2016

LITRES PER YEAR
10,000

SISTER GIN
Limited edition Barrel-Aged Garden Swift

Perfect pours

GIN AND TONIC

Garden Swift 50ml
Unflavoured tonic water 125ml
Orange to garnish

Put a slice of orange (blood orange is good) into a large wine glass containing lots of ice. Add the gin and top with tonic water.

THE CHAMOIS

Garden Swift 25ml
Genepi (Alpine herbal liqueur) 25ml
Cloudy apple juice 100ml
Sage leaf to garnish

Pour everything into a large wine glass with lots of ice and garnish with a fresh sage leaf.

www.capreolusdistillery.co.uk   01285 644477
The Mount, Park View, Cirencester, Gloucestershire, GL7 2JG

Tasting notes

A multilayered gin with succulent sweet orange to the fore, floral whiffs and warm, spicy and herbal notes. Intense essential oils mean the gin clouds over and swirls hazily around ice cubes.

ABV 47%

3 Ramsbury Gin

This is the very definition of 'single estate gin' and is made from scratch on Stockclose Farm near Marlborough. The team even distil the base spirit from wheat grown on the farm.

It's a sustainable system: heat is generated by a biomass boiler, waste goes to a reed-bed filter and the estate's own water is used.

Fresh quince joins the classic botanicals of juniper, angelica and orris root along with dried citrus peel, cinnamon and liquorice. And everything is distilled in a state-of-the-art 43-plate copper column still.

DISTILLERY
Ramsbury Distillery

ESTABLISHED
2015

GIN LAUNCHED
2017

DISTILLERY TOURS
Available

GINS SOLD
On site

Perfect pours

GIN AND TONIC

Pour a large measure of Ramsbury Gin over plenty of large ice cubes, top with premium Indian tonic and garnish with a thin slice of apple, pear or quince.

RAMSBURY MARTINI

Shake a large measure of Ramsbury Gin with a small dash of vermouth over ice. Strain into a martini glass.

www.ramsbury.com   07841 444705
Stockclose Farm, Aldbourne, Wiltshire, SN8 2NN

Tasting notes

Very dry and clean, with a herbaceous quality, there's a fresh, grassy edge to the aroma of this gin. Complex notes include liquorice and the pear-apple flavour of quince on the taste.

ABV 40%

4 6 O'clock Gin

6 O'clock Gin, in its stunning Bristol blue glass bottle, is named after a family tradition of indulging in a G&T at exactly 6 O'clock each evening.

Head distiller Edward founded Bramley & Gage in 1988, originally making fruit liqueurs in south Devon. He developed an old family gin recipe in order to create Bramley & Gage's first sloe gin, and this London dry was later perfected by his children, Michael and Felicity (who now run the business).

The resulting 6 O'clock is traditional in style with juniper aromas sitting alongside other carefully selected botanicals including elderflower, winter savory and orange peel.

DISTILLERY
6 O'clock Gin

ESTABLISHED
1988

GIN LAUNCHED
2010

LITRES PER YEAR
70,000

SISTER GINS
Brunel Edition
Damson Gin

DISTILLERY TOURS
Available

Perfect pours

GIN AND TONIC

Use plenty of ice, good tonic and a lemon twist for a refreshing, classic G&T. As the clock strikes 6pm, naturally ...

FLORODORA

Use 6 O'clock Gin as a cocktail ingredient in a Florodora - long and refreshing with warming ginger spice.

www.6oclockgin.com   01454 418046
Ashville Park, Short Way, Thornbury, Bristol, BS35 3UU

Tasting notes

A gin of true elegance: soft,
crisp and clean, leading with
juniper before revealing
further notes of elderflower
and subtle spice with a citrus
twist on the finish.

ABV 43%

5 Wōden Gin

Wōden is crafted at Bristol's Psychopomp Microdistillery by Danny Walker and Liam Hirt, who started out making gin as a hobby in Liam's basement.

Word soon got out, demand grew and the pair turned pro in 2015, establishing themselves as a renowned and cult distiller on Bristol's burgeoning spirits scene.

Wōden is an Anglo-Saxon god (Wednesday is named after him) and, myth has it, a 'psychopomp' or guiding spirit.

Botanicals include cassia, fresh pink grapefruit zest and fennel seeds in this classic London dry gin with a notably clean and fresh character.

DISTILLERY
Psychopomp Microdistillery

ESTABLISHED
2013

GIN LAUNCHED
2014

LITRES PER YEAR
10,000

SISTER GINS
4 limited edition seasonal gins a year plus an Old Tom

DISTILLERY TOURS
Available

GINS SOLD
On site

Perfect pours

GIN AND TONIC

Wōden Gin 50ml
Fever-Tree tonic 100ml
Pink grapefruit to garnish

Pour the gin into a tall glass with ice and top with tonic. Garnish with a wedge of pink grapefruit.

WEDNESDAY MARTINI

Wōden Gin 60ml
Dry vermouth 10ml
Grapefruit to garnish

Stir both over ice and strain into a martini glass. Garnish with grapefruit zest.

www.microdistillery.co.uk   07511 934675
145 St Michael's Hill, Bristol, BS2 8DB

Tasting notes

Fresh, appealing aroma of juniper
and citrus peel with a light aniseed
note from fennel seed. Clean and
crisp on the palate with a subtle
twist of cinnamon-like spice.

ABV 40%

PSYCHOPOMP MICRO-DISTILLERY

'WODEN'

DISTILLED CRAFT GIN

70CL

ALC40%VOL

GIN
WŌ
Craft Distilled
PSYCHOPOMP
145 St Michaels Hill,
Bristol BS2 8DB

6 GinJar Twisted Rhubarb & Ginger Gin

Somerset's GinJar Drinks Company grew out of a belief that life should be *'pleasantly twisted'*. That, and founder Chris Jefferies' passion for making drinks: he was producing homemade beer, cider and wine (from 36 vines in his garden) before even thinking about gin.

Chris now creates five gins, each label reflecting a seasonal flavour and seasonal sport. This particular spirit started life *'in the garage,'* according to Chris, who says: *'With all of our gins we had a few hits and misses before we pleased more than just our friends'*.

DISTILLERY
GinJar Drinks Company

ESTABLISHED
2015

GIN LAUNCHED
2016

LITRES PER YEAR
600

SISTER GINS
GinJar Twisted Elderflower

GinJar Twisted Burnt Orange

Perfect pours

CLASSIC SERVE

GinJar Twisted Rhubarb & Ginger Gin topped with chilled premium ginger beer and garnished with a slice of fresh lime.

TWISTED FIZZ

GinJar Twisted Rhubarb & Ginger Gin 50ml
Lemon juice 10ml
Sugar syrup 10-15ml
Prosecco to top up
Mint leaves to garnish

Pour the gin, lemon juice and syrup into a glass with ice. Stir and garnish with mint leaves.

www.ginjar.co.uk   07909 737373

Unit 21, Winchester Farm, Draycott Road, Cheddar, Somerset, BS27 3RP

Tasting notes

Starts with a rich fruity aroma of red berries and stewed rhubarb, then on mid-palate the ginger kicks in - subtle but warming - before juicy fruitiness takes over again.

ABV 40%

Small Batch Infused Gin

BATCH   GJRG/001

Refreshingly Twisted

70cl   40% ALC/VOL

7 El8hteen Gin

Retired process engineer Leigh Kearle is the distiller behind this taste-of-Somerset gin, and he's exacting about each stage of its creation. All of Leigh's gins are made from scratch, starting with a sugar-beet base spirit which provides extra smoothness.

The spirit is then redistilled with its botanicals in copper pot alembic stills.

El8hteen balances vibrant juniper in a classic London dry style with gorgeously subtle orchard-fruit scents and flavours, a soft spicy hint and lightly nutty finish.

You may spot a light cloudy haze to it once diluted as, in order to deliver full flavours, this gin is not chill-filtered.

DISTILLERY
El8hteen Gin

ESTABLISHED
2016

GIN LAUNCHED
2016

LITRES PER YEAR
18,355

SISTER GINS
Lemon Gin
Coconut Gin
Liqueur

DISTILLERY TOURS
Available

GINS SOLD
On site

Perfect pours

GIN AND TONIC
Serve with Double Dutch Skinny Tonic Water or a light alternative. Garnish with a slice of fresh apple.

ALTERNATIVE GARNISHES
Replace the apple with a slice of pear, pink grapefruit or a wedge of nectarine – but never lemon or lime.

www.18gin.co.uk   07789 222692

The Hive, Woolmersdon, North Petherton, Somerset, TA5 2BP

Floral top note of apple blossom scent with plenty of classic juniper on the palate, alongside more apple, subtle shades of anise and ground macadamia nuts.

ABV 42%

E18HTEEN
18GIN

Somerset Premium Gin
delicately distilled by hand in
small batches and infused with
the finest countryside botanicals
to deliver exquisite smoothness.

70cl · 42% Vol

8 Newton House Gin

After ten years restoring Newton House in Somerset, and inspired by the plants in its walled garden, Robin and Jane Cannon created a gin which is as fresh and inviting as a fine West Country summer day.

The estate covers 60 acres and the natural spring water which flows through it is also used in the creation of this spirit.

Botanicals include mint, bergamot, grapefruit, peaches and blueberries and the gin is distilled in copper stills in the former carpenter's workshop. The result is a distinctively fragrant and crisp gin, delicate with a lingering finish.

DISTILLERY
Newton Drinks

ESTABLISHED
2017

GIN LAUNCHED
2017

LITRES PER YEAR
50,000

SISTER GINS
Damson Gin
Mulled Gin

DISTILLERY TOURS
Available

GINS SOLD
On site

Perfect pours

GIN AND TONIC

Newton House Gin 25ml
Fever-Tree Tonic 100ml
Mint leaf to garnish

Put ice and a slice of lime in a wide-bowled glass. Add the gin and the tonic. Garnish with a lightly bruised mint leaf.

NEWTONI COCKTAIL

Newton House Gin 50ml
Elderflower cordial 15ml
Freshly squeezed lemon juice 50ml
Cucumber 2 slices
Sea salt a pinch
Dill a sprig

Shake everything over ice and double strain into a cocktail glass. Garnish with a sprig of dill.

www.newtonhousegin.co.uk   01935 471388

Newton House, Newton Surmaville, Yeovil, Somerset, BA20 2RX

Tasting notes

There's a clean, zesty air to this gin, with its subtle dab of fresh mint and clear citrus notes. Lightly peachy on the mid-palate, it lingers elegantly on the finish.

ABV 43.2%

9 Conker Spirit Dorset Dry Gin

Distilled in Bournemouth from ten carefully selected botanicals, Conker is made in two 60 litre alembic pot stills.

It was created in spring 2014 by Rupert Holloway whose inspiration was the fresh and herbaceous Dorset countryside.

This is a classic London dry but local botanicals such as hand-picked gorse flowers, elderberries and marsh samphire deliver appealing layers of flavour. The local provenance continues in the use of New Forest spring water.

The result is a bright and vivacious gin, not as bone dry as some, with fascinating complexity.

DISTILLERY
Conker Spirit

ESTABLISHED
2014

GIN LAUNCHED
2014

LITRES PER YEAR
35,000

GINS SOLD
On site

Perfect pours

GIN AND TONIC

Dorset Dry Gin 50ml
Indian tonic water 200ml
Lime to garnish

Pour the gin into a glass with lots of ice. Top with tonic and garnish with a twist of lime peel.

COLD BREW G&T

Dorset Dry Gin 25ml
Conker Cold Brew Coffee Liqueur 25ml
Indian tonic 200ml
Fresh orange wheel to garnish

Serve in a glass with ice. Mix and garnish with a fresh orange wheel.

www.conkerspirit.co.uk   01202 430384
Unit 3, 16a Inverleigh Road, Bournemouth, Dorset, BH6 5HA

Tasting notes

Bright, bold juniper and fresh
limey citrus on aroma and palate,
with a softer, subtly sweet hint
of blueberry rounding out the
flavour. Dry, tangy and clean
long-finish.

ABV 40%

10 Pothecary Gin

Pothecary's unique character derives from the use of bold botanicals which include lavender for aroma, tilia flowers for honeyed and fresh notes, and black mulberries for a ripe fruitiness.

The ingredients come from around the world and are all organic or wild foraged – the gin has now been certified organic by the Soil Association.

It's made by a multi-shot technique, each botanical distilled separately before being blended together and cut with New Forest spring water.

DISTILLERY
Soapbox Spirits

ESTABLISHED
2016

GIN LAUNCHED
2016

LITRES PER YEAR
6,000 - 8,000

SISTER GINS
Limited Edition Sicilian Blend

Limited Edition Thai Blend

Perfect pours

GIN AND TONIC

Serve with standard Indian tonic water at a ratio of 1:2 gin to tonic. Garnish with a thin twist of lemon peel.

CLASSIC COCKTAILS

Pothecary makes for an interesting and floral take on the classic Negroni or Dry Martini with vermouth.

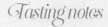
Tasting notes

The inviting, summery aroma of lavender is followed by plenty of citrus and supported by bright juniper. A lightly oily, honeyed hint ends rich and smooth with a note of juicy sweetness.

ABV 44.8%

11 Northmoor Gin

Made at the newly founded Exmoor Distillery, Northmoor is named after the eponymous historic estate nestled in steep wooded valleys on the southern edge of Exmoor.

John and Nicola Smith recently launched the distillery and are producing a gin which packs a punch at 44 per cent while still retaining a well balanced and smooth finish.

In addition to traditional juniper and angelica root, the Smiths employ citrus and spice botanicals in a gin that can be enjoyed neat over ice, in a classic G&T or as a premium base for cocktails.

DISTILLERY
Exmoor Distillery

ESTABLISHED
2018

GIN LAUNCHED
2018

GINS SOLD
On site

Perfect pours

GIN AND TONIC
Serve over ice with your favourite tonic and a slice of fresh lime.

GRAPEFRUIT G&T
Replace the lime with a slice of fresh pink grapefruit to bring out different notes in the gin.

www.exmoordistillery.co.uk   01398 323488
Unit 5, Barle Enterprise Centre, Dulverton, Somerset, TA22 9BF

Tasting notes

This is a bold gin with a
compelling aroma and flavour, and
bright juniper shining through.
Expect juicy citrus and spicy-
pepper notes to the flavour and a
rounded and lingering finish.

ABV 44%

12 Wicked Wolf Exmoor Gin

Pat Patel and Julie Heap launched Wicked Wolf in 2015 after two years of experimenting with gin.

The pair eventually settled on 11 key botanicals, each individually distilled before being blended. Using a copper alembic still at their distillery in Brendon, Exmoor, the gin is crafted in 100 litre batches. It's also filtered at each stage for smoothness.

This contemporary spirit reflects Pat's favoured bold flavours and also reveals Asian influences: kaffir lime leaves, cardamom, lemongrass and hibiscus all feature in a gin of subtlety and elegance.

Perfect paired with spiced dishes.

DISTILLERY
The Old Chapel Brendon

ESTABLISHED
2015

GIN LAUNCHED
2015

LITRES PER YEAR
25,000

SISTER GINS
**Full Moon
Silver Bullet**

Perfect pours

GIN AND TONIC
Serve with quality tonic, plenty of ice and a slice of pink grapefruit or lime.

WILD THYMES
For a more savoury note, serve with quality tonic, ice and a slice of lime plus a sprig of thyme.

www.wickedwolfgin.com 01598 741357
The Old Chapel, Brendon, Devon, EX35 6PT

Tasting notes

Top notes of fresh citrus and a
distinct scent of kaffir lime leaf is
interwoven with more traditional
juniper and coriander. Fresh and
slightly peppery on the finish.

ABV 42%

**WICKED
WOLF**®

SMALL BATCH HANDCRAFTED
EXMOOR GIN

70 cl   alc. 42% vol

13 Copper Frog Gin

The founder and distiller of Copper Frog, Simon Hughes, has always been fascinated by traditional skills and, after making alcoholic ginger beer and rhubarb vodka, turned his hand to gin in 2017.

The result is Copper Frog, which is crafted in small batches in Exmouth. The gin is steam-distilled in a beautiful Portuguese still named Jenny, using pure filtered water from Exmoor National Park and high quality botanicals. These include lime, pink grapefruit and pink peppercorns for a smooth, well-flavoured gin which, according to Simon, is spot on for matching with seafood – as well as enjoying on its own.

DISTILLERY
Copper Frog Distilling

ESTABLISHED
2017

GIN LAUNCHED
2017

LITRES PER YEAR
2,500

Perfect pours

GIN AND TONIC

Pour a double measure over a small amount of ice and top with Fever-Tree Light Tonic. Garnish with two quarter slices of pink grapefruit.

COPPER FROG'S FRENCH 75

Take a double measure of gin, plus sugar syrup and grapefruit juice to taste. Shake over ice and strain into a cocktail glass. Top up with champagne and garnish with a twist of pink grapefruit.

www.copperfrogdistilling.co.uk   07971 554376
Exmouth, Devon

Tasting notes

The fruity aroma of juicy lime
and pink grapefruit is followed
by a smooth, rounded and fresh
flavour and texture. Finally, the
warm spice of pink peppercorn
comes through and lingers on
the palate.

ABV 42%

14 Thunderflower Gin

This newly launched Devon gin is named after the tiny white flower that sometimes grows on thatched cottage roofs and which, according to legend, wards off storms and witchcraft.

Happily, purely good spirits remain in this micro-batch gin which is produced in one-shot distillation runs, with vapour infusion of the botanical mix.

One for the gin traditionalist looking for a classic London dry, expect earthy notes with a spicy edge as a result of botanicals such as cassia bark, fresh sage leaves, heather, and green and smoked black cardamom.

DISTILLERY
Thunderflower

ESTABLISHED
2017

GIN LAUNCHED
2018

LITRES PER YEAR
5,000

Perfect pours

GIN AND TONIC

Thunderflower Gin 40ml
Lamb & Watt Original Tonic Water 90ml
Lemon half slice

Take a short glass full of ice and add half a slice of lemon. Pour in the gin and tonic and give it a gentle stir.

ON THE ROCKS

Thunderflower makes a good sipping gin when served in a short glass over large square cubes of ice.

www.thunderflower.co.uk   01626 374055

60 Higher Brimley Road, Teignmouth, Devon, TQ14 8JU

Tasting notes

An earthy, juniper-driven gin
that's dry and complex with
distinctive, well-balanced
spiciness. Especially unusual
is the note of smoked black
cardamom and twist of
pink peppercorn on the
lingering finish.

ABV 42%

15 Start Point

Start Point Lighthouse symbolises the voyages of Salcombe's historic fruit schooners to collect the exotic goods which inspired this premium gin.

Co-founders Angus Lugsdin and Howard Davies met in their teens as sailing instructors in Salcombe and created this state-of-the-art distillery; one of the only distilleries in the world directly accessible by boat. At its heart is the handsome 450 litre copper still named Provident.

Naturally soft water from Dartmoor is used along with 13 botanicals which include Macedonian juniper, English coriander seed, and fresh red grapefruit, lemon and lime.

DISTILLERY
Salcombe Distilling Co.

ESTABLISHED
2016

GIN LAUNCHED
2016

LITRES PER YEAR
100,000

SISTER GINS
The Voyager Series

DISTILLERY TOURS
Available

GINS SOLD
On site

Perfect pours

GIN AND TONIC

Pour a large measure of Start Point and 150ml of premium tonic into a large glass filled with plenty of ice. Garnish with a slice of red grapefruit.

ST CLAIR

Start Point 25ml
St Germain elderflower liqueur 25ml
Red grapefruit juice 20ml
Soda water 70ml

Shake ingredients over ice and strain into a flute. Top up with chilled soda water and garnish with a twist of red grapefruit peel.

www.salcombegin.com   01548 288180

The Boathouse, 28-30 Island Street, Salcombe, Devon, TQ8 8DP

Tasting notes

A classic, super smooth London dry gin with scented juniper, herbal notes and an emphasis on citrus (particularly red grapefruit) for a whistle-clean finish.

ABV 44%

16 Barbican Botanics Gin

Just seven botanicals are used in the crafting of Barbican Botanics Gin, but each of them – from milk thistle root to fennel seed – play a key role in delivering distinctive aromas and flavours.

The distillation process is extremely slow, which helps to produce a super smooth, almost creamy finish. This is a true 'small batch gin', distilled in a 30 litre traditional copper alembic still.

Although robust at 45 per cent, its well-balanced finish is much softer and more rounded than you might expect in a gin of this strength.

DISTILLERY
Barbican Botanics Gin

ESTABLISHED
2017

GIN LAUNCHED
2017

LITRES PER YEAR
2,000

GINS SOLD
On site

Perfect pours

GIN AND TONIC

Barbican Botanics Gin 50ml
Premium tonic water 150ml
Lemon to garnish
Star anise to garnish

Put a slice of lemon and a star anise into a copa glass filled with ice. Add gin and top with tonic water.

STRAIGHT UP

Enjoy served straight over large chunks of ice for an impressively smooth sipping spirit.

www.littleginbox.com   02087 989278
38 New Street, Plymouth, Devon, PL1 2NA

Tasting notes

After bold and aromatic juniper, detect an earthy middle note from the milk thistle root. A lingering round finish features a fresh and aniseedy hint of fennel seed.

ABV 45%

17 Trevethan Cornish Craft Gin

The original Trevethan gin was crafted by Norman Trevethan in 1929 in a simple copper pot still on the Port Eliot estate in Cornwall.

The gin was relaunched in 2014 and remains true to the original recipe – especially its use of Cornish ingredients such as elderflower and gorse flower.

Head distiller John Hall refined the distillation for the modern version and has created a spirit with powerful fragrance, complex flavours and a smooth texture.

DISTILLERY
Trevethan Distillery

ESTABLISHED
2015

GIN LAUNCHED
2015

LITRES PER YEAR
62,400

SISTER GINS
Trevethan Honey Oak Gin

Trevethan Chauffeur's Reserve

DISTILLERY TOURS
Available

GINS SOLD
On site

Perfect pours

THE 1929

Trevethan Cornish Craft Gin 50ml
Cucumber tonic 100ml
Cucumber to garnish
Lemon to garnish
Basil to garnish

Pour ingredients into a glass filled with ice and garnish with cucumber, lemon and basil.

GIN AND TONIC

Serve over ice with a naturally light tonic, twist of orange peel and a small sprig of rosemary.

www.trevethandistillery.com   07951 685724

Unit 20a, Prideaux Close, Tamar View, Saltash, Cornwall, PL12 6LD

Tasting notes

Expect a powerful citrus aroma and
complex flavours of juniper, orange
and lemon with hints of vanilla and
cardamom. Soft and smooth, it's almost
lightly oily in texture.

ABV 43%

18 The Wrecking Coast Clotted Cream Gin

The founders of this Cornish distillery love gin, but before the gin revolution, their chosen tipple was fine whisky.

Avian Sandercock, Craig Penn and Steve Wharton's passion was to create a gin that would shine in a G&T, be bold as a cocktail base and, most importantly, stand on its own as that rarest of drinks – a sipping gin.

To retain the delicate flavours and textures of clotted cream, Rodda's Cornish clotted cream is vacuum distilled separately.

Twelve robust botanicals with juniper and coriander at the lead are precision-distilled in high-tech apparatus to create a spicy base which envelopes the cream and delivers a gin loaded with flavours and complex textures.

DISTILLERY
The Wrecking Coast Distillery

ESTABLISHED
2015

GIN LAUNCHED
2016

LITRES PER YEAR
20,000

SISTER GINS
Scurvy Gin
Navy Strength
Honey Sloe Gin

Perfect pours

GIN AND TONIC

Allow sliced or muddled fresh strawberries to sit on the neat gin before adding ice and a quality Indian tonic.

ALTERNATIVE GARNISHES

Red berries work exceptionally well, strawberries or raspberries making the cream notes shine. Use blueberries with lemon zest as a worthy alternative.

www.thewreckingcoastdistillery.com

Unit 2, Pentire Workshops, Delabole, Cornwall, PL33 9BA

Tasting notes

A very smooth and rounded
gin, almost creamy in texture,
though not remotely sweet.
Juniper shines through while
other botanicals add freshness
and complexity.

ABV 44%

19 Tarquin's Cornish Dry Gin

In 2013, Paris-trained chef Tarquin Leadbetter, then just 23, established the first new distillery in Cornwall for more than a hundred years.

After many trials, Tarquin created his popular gin which is now produced in four stills – the 250 litre Tamara, Senara and Tressa, along with newer 500 litre Ferrara.

This is a contemporary, Cornish take on a London dry gin which uses violet flowers and orange zest among the botanicals.

Each of the distinctive bottles is wax sealed, labelled and signed by hand.

DISTILLERY
Southwestern Distillery

ESTABLISHED
2013

GIN LAUNCHED
2013

SISTER GINS
The SeaDog Navy Gin

Tarquin's British Blackberry Gin

GINS SOLD
On site

Perfect pours

GIN AND TONIC

Tarquin's Cornish Dry Gin 50ml
Fever-Tree Mediterranean Tonic 100ml
Pink grapefruit to garnish
Fresh thyme to garnish

Serve in a glass with plenty of ice. Garnish with pink grapefruit and fresh thyme.

CORNISH GARDEN SMASH

Tarquin's Cornish Dry Gin 50ml
Fresh lemon juice 20ml
Elderflower syrup 20ml
White vermouth 10ml
Pastis a dash
Cucumber 4cm slice, cubed
Herbs and edible flowers to garnish

Mix ingredients in a glass with ice and garnish with herbs and flowers.

www.tarquinsgin.com   01841 540121
Higher Trevibban Farm, Wadebridge, Cornwall, PL27 7SH

Tasting notes

This is a fragrant gin with a floral note to the aroma. Classic juniper sweeps in on first taste, with fresh and clean citrus on the finish.

ABV 42%

20 Curio Rock Samphire Gin

You only have to imagine waves crashing onto the rocks in west Cornwall and the salty tang in the air to get a taste of what inspired Rubina and William Tyler-Street to create this highly individual gin.

The key botanical, along with juniper, is rock samphire – the edible wild herb that clings to coastal clifftops – which imparts citrus, peppery and herbal tones to the spirit. Kombu seaweed adds a savoury saline note.

With fresh, mainly hand-foraged botanicals and pristine Cornish spring water, this is a wake-up call to the palate.

DISTILLERY
Curio Spirits

ESTABLISHED
2014

GIN LAUNCHED
2014

LITRES PER YEAR
40,000

SISTER GINS
Fly Navy Gin
Tyler-Street Gin

Perfect pours

GIN AND TONIC

Serve over ice with Franklin Light Tonic. Garnish with a slice of lime, a few juniper berries and a sprig of rock samphire.

CURIO ORIENTAL SUNSET

Curio Rock Samphire Gin 2 parts
Triple sec 1 part
Lemon juice
Lychees whole

Shake and pour over ice into a highball tumbler. Garnish with lychees.

www.curiospiritscompany.co.uk   07940 730958
Trenance, Mullion, Cornwall, TR12 7HB

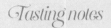

Tasting notes

Citrus fresh with dried herbs, white
pepper and a light salty-savoury
note which conjures up refreshing
sea-salt spray and iodine.

ABV 41%

21 Caspyn Cornish Dry Gin

Pocketful of Stones, the distillery which makes Caspyn, came about when two brothers sat down in the cellar of a London pub and tinkered with a tiny copper still. Their aim was to create a gin which reflected their Cornish surroundings, the great outdoors and the ocean.

The resulting Cornish Dry is crisp, invigorating and distinctly floral with hints of exotic botanicals which include lemongrass, hibiscus, citrus, lemon verbena and Japanese tea.

DISTILLERY
Pocketful of Stones Distillers

ESTABLISHED
2016

GIN LAUNCHED
2016

LITRES PER YEAR
8,000

SISTER GINS
Caspyn Midsummer Gin

Newlyn Coombe Damson Gin

DISTILLERY TOURS
Available

Perfect pours

COSMO DAISY

Caspyn Cornish Dry Gin 50ml
Lemon juice 25ml
Sugar syrup 15ml
Orange curacao 15ml
Raspberries 3

Muddle the raspberries in a shaker, add other ingredients and ice. Shake and double strain into a chilled martini glass and garnish with orange.

GIN AND TONIC

Serve over ice with a premium tonic. Garnish with a twist of orange to let the flavours and aromas of the gin sing.

Tasting notes

Lemon verbena carries through
on the scent and there's a
dry lemon-sherbet freshness
and hint of tea leaves in this
complex, fresh-tasting gin.

ABV 40%

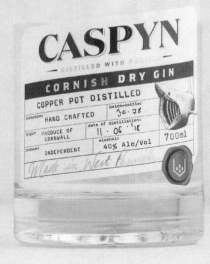

GIN HAUNTS

Exceptional bars which serve premium
small-batch gins with style

22 The Painswick

Kemps Lane, Painswick, Gloucestershire, GL6 6YB

E qual measures of luxury, laid-back vibes and quirkiness make this Gloucestershire country house hotel a unique find.

Local Cotswolds Gin takes centre stage on a drinks list which brims with unusual spirits from near and far. The team have clearly had fun crafting concoctions such as the Rococo Garden, a cocktail inspired by a luscious local garden in Painswick. It features fresh raspberries, Bombay gin, Chambord, lime and rosemary syrup.

'The Sunday Times' Ultimate Hotel of The Year 2016'

As it was *The Sunday Times'* Ultimate Hotel of the Year 2016, it would be a shame not to experience The Painswick in all its incarnations. Go all out and book a treatment at the spa before a signature G&T and dinner in the restaurant with views over the valley.

ESTABLISHED
2016

GINS
13

SEATS
36

FOOD
Served

HOUSE GIN
Available

www.thepainswick.co.uk   01452 813688

23 The Bell Inn

Bell Lane, Selsley, Gloucestershire, GL5 5JY

If you're looking for a country pub that ticks all the boxes, this Cotswolds inn is a strong contender. A top-notch dining pub with seriously good grub, fine wines and a bountiful bill of local ales is what you'd hope for – and find. What you might not expect is a dedicated gin tasting room with 90 varieties of the spirit.

Visit the dedicated gin tasting room with 90 varieties of the spirit'

Nine local gins are complemented by picks from across the globe which have been carefully selected to provide a full range of palate-pleasing botanicals.

Experience the gins at regular tasting events (bespoke sessions available), swing by to chat to a distiller at one of the meet-the-producer evenings, or buy bottles and gin hampers to take home.

ESTABLISHED
2015

GINS
90

SEATS
55

FOOD
Served

HOUSE GIN
Available

www.thebellinnselsley.com 01453 753801

24 Chewton Glen Hotel & Spa

New Forest, Hampshire, BH25 6QS

The Marryat Bar, with its traditional decor of dark wood and leather, is the oldest room in this historic manor. And, with 28 exquisite gins in its stonking spirits collection, should be the first port of call for any gin lover.

Recommended are the Conker Pink made with Conker Gin from Dorset, or the house speciality, Hot G&T, crafted with vegetable gin from nearby Soapbox Spirits. All of the G&Ts are served with garnishes grown in the kitchen garden and, on fine days, can also be sipped alfresco while overlooking the manicured croquet lawn.

ESTABLISHED
1966

GINS
28

SEATS
40

FOOD
Served

HOUSE GIN
Available

'Take a gin course or cocktail masterclass at the cookery school'

If you're up for expanding your palate, take a gin course or cocktail masterclass at the cookery school.

www.chewtonglen.com   01425 275341

25 The Swan Wedmore

Cheddar Road, Wedmore, Somerset, BS28 4EQ

If you're always on the lookout for cosy, characterful pubs in which to spend evenings sipping cocktails and dining on award winning food, be sure to scribble 'The Swan' in your little black book.

This country inn, led by Tom Blake (formerly of River Cottage) with head chef Jack Stoodley, champions local, seasonal and artisan produce. The fact that the team cures their own bacon gives an idea of their commitment to quality and provenance.

'The house Negroni is highly recommended'

The drinks are taken just as seriously and the 30-strong gin list is augmented by regular tasting evenings and a month-long gin festival. We'd recommend cosying up next to the wood burner with a house Negroni while deciding which of the artfully chosen collection of cocktails to hit up next.

ESTABLISHED
2011

GINS
30

SEATS
106

FOOD
Served

HOUSE GIN
Available

26 Brazz

Castle Bow, Taunton, Somerset, TA1 1NF

Brazz is the funky (and slightly naughty) younger sibling of Taunton's grand Castle Hotel. A fairly recent refurb has seen it transformed into the city's go-to spot for chic shenanigans. Perch at the gleaming bar or cocoon yourself in one of the plush peacock-blue velvet booths and work your way through the creative cocktail list.

The team switch up the drinks regularly and popular signatures include the Brazz Vesper Martini, The Rose, Gin O'Clock and The Mystery. As you'd expect, there's also a pleasing selection of South West gins on offer.

'Perch at the gleaming bar or cocoon yourself in one of the plush peacock-blue velvet booths'

The food from exec chef Liam Finnegan and brigade is equally noteworthy, so make sure you stick around for supper.

ESTABLISHED
1998

GINS
10

SEATS
50

FOOD
Served

HOUSE GIN
Available

www.brazz.co.uk   01823 252000

27 Dunster Castle Hotel

5 High Street, Dunster, Minehead, Somerset, TA24 6SF

Set at the foot of Dunster Castle, this Grade II-listed hotel combines traditional heritage with a playful steampunk twist at its Gin and Tiffin bar. An alembic copper still provides a funky centrepiece, with chic copper pipework creeping out over the walls to frame artwork.

Pair your pick of the hundred-strong gin list with a selection of tiffin (small dishes inspired by the British Raj), for a unique interpretation of the classic G&T.

Adventurous palates can choose one of six gin flights: the Local includes three gins served on a handmade wooden tray, which showcases South West stunners such as Wicked Wolf and Newton House.

"Pair your pick of the hundred strong list with a selection of tiffin"

Also recommended is the signature Southside cocktail which is a little like a Gin Mojito.

ESTABLISHED
2016

GINS
100

SEATS
70

FOOD
Served

www.dunstercastlehotel.co.uk   01643 823030

28 Thomas Carr Seafood & Grill

59 High Street, Ilfracombe, Devon, EX34 9QB

Thomas Carr Seafood & Grill is the new restaurant and bar from the Michelin-starred chef. It's also the chilled out little brother to fine dining HQ, The Olive Room.

It's a comfortable spot where original Victorian features in the restaurant sit cheek-by-jowl with a modern bar and Mediterranean-style courtyard.

'Let the team craft you a bespoke, flight of three gins'

Pair locally landed and line-caught seafood with one of the 43 gins or start the evening with a gin flight at the bar: tell the team the flavours you favour and let them craft a bespoke flight of three different gins.

Regular cocktail masterclasses offer a fun way to spend an afternoon with friends – and you'll get to drink your own creations and concoctions.

ESTABLISHED
2018

GINS
43

SEATS
70

FOOD
Served

HOUSE GIN
Available

www.thomascarrdining.co.uk   01271 555005

29 Watersmeet Hotel

The Esplanade, Woolacombe, Devon, EX34 7EB

Life's a beach at this fabulous find for gin lovers who also like to feel sand between their toes. With its awesome setting overlooking the golden shore and surf-central waves of Woolacombe, there are few more beautiful places to apply oneself to the job of working through a 13-strong gin list.

Naturally, you'll also want to mix up the imbibing with a spot of sunning on the lawn, swimming in the oceanside pool and chilling on the terrace.

'For gin lovers who also like to feel sand between their toes'

If you're visiting for the evening, kick off with a pre-dinner gin cocktail before dining in the two AA rosette-awarded Pavilion Restaurant where head chef John Prince cooks up fine dishes using locally sourced meat and fish.

ESTABLISHED
2003

GINS
13

SEATS
80

FOOD
Served

HOUSE GIN
Available

www.watersmeethotel.co.uk   01271 870333

30 Saunton Sands Hotel

Saunton Road, Saunton, Braunton, Devon, EX33 1LQ

The terrace of this art deco hotel on the north Devon coast must be one of the most stunning gin-sipping spots in the UK.

Eleven gins feature on the bar list; go hyper local with an Exmoor-distilled Wicked Wolf and tonic, or choose from a raft of craft UK gins presented in their recommended serve style. Alternatively (if it's that kind of evening), explore the signature cocktails which reflect the art deco period: the most popular is a White Lady, made with Plymouth Gin.

> *Explore the signature cocktails which reflect the art deco period*

Contrary to what you might assume, it's not necessary to be a hotel resident to enjoy the well crafted drinks, fabulous setting or two AA rosette restaurant, so this is a bit of an insider's find.

ESTABLISHED
1977

GINS
11

SEATS
380

FOOD
Served

HOUSE GIN
Available

www.sauntonsands.co.uk   01271 890212

31 SQ Bar and Restaurant

3 Exeter Road, Braunton, Devon, EX33 2JT

When the sun's out in north Devon and the desire for gin arises, the roof terrace at SQ is quite the spot. However, don't let the weather dictate your visit to this smart establishment in the centre of Braunton village, as the contemporary bar is equally pleasing.

Elegant surrounds are matched by an impressive list of gin cocktails and, if you ask the bartenders for their fave aperitif, they'll recommend a simple but elegant Gin Fizz (gin, fresh lime, sugar syrup and prosecco) every time. Another house fave is the quintessentially English Earl Grey Fizz.

'A house fave is the quintessentially English Earl Grey Fizz'

Sign up for a full day of spirited action at a SQ Gin Day and try up to 30 different gins, each served with the perfect garnish and tonic to let the botanicals sing.

ESTABLISHED
2014

GINS
25

SEATS
120

FOOD
Served

HOUSE GIN
Available

www.sqdining.co.uk   01271 815900

WRECKING
COAST
DISTILLERY

PROUD SPONSOR
OF THE

INDEPENDENT
GIN
GUIDE

THEWRECKINGCOASTDISTILLERY.COM

32 Bar 62

62 Boutport Street, Barnstaple, Devon, EX31 1HG

This rather grand old building may once have been a bank, but nowadays you're more likely to visit for its vaulted collection of artisan gins.

Gin lovers will want to cash in on Bar 62's South West Gin Tour: a virtual tipsy trip across the region which involves the sampling of eight different gins with unique garnishes.

The first stop takes in the terroir of Exmoor (Wicked Wolf Gin with orange, lavender and Luscombe tonic), while the final destination is the Cornish coast where Curio Gin is matched with coriander, lime and Luscombe tonic.

'Cash in on Bar 62's South West gin tour'

Alternatively, choose from 21 gins while picking at a Grazing Crate, or follow your gin indulgences with a more substantial supper next door at 62 The Bank.

ESTABLISHED
2016

GINS
21

SEATS
52

FOOD
Served

---

www.62thebank.co.uk   01271 324446

33 Paschoe House

Bow, Crediton, Devon, EX17 6JT

With features dating back to the 13th century, Paschoe House holds a whole history of tales from times gone by within its ancient walls. Today, however, you'll find the beautiful building thriving in its latest guise as a luxurious country house hotel.

'Sip a signature cocktail on the South Terrace before strolling in the walled garden'

The first port of call for any visitor must be the Library Bar which, alongside a huge stuffed ostrich, features a choice collection of 19 different gins (many local). Sip a signature cocktail – recommended is a Bramble – on the South Terrace, before taking a stroll in the Victorian walled garden.

Sign up for one of the popular gin experiences and be sure to stick around for dinner at the beautiful fine dining restaurant which features in the 2019 *Michelin Guide.*

ESTABLISHED
2017

GINS
19

SEATS
40

FOOD
Served

HOUSE GIN
Available

www.paschoehouse.co.uk   01363 84244

34 The Oddfellows

60 New North Road, Exeter, Devon, EX4 4EP

This Exeter stalwart has everything you'd want in an indie dining pub: delicious and hearty food, great beer and, best of all, an entire shelf of South West gins.

'Matched with seasonal ingredients in an Instagrammable collection of cocktails'

Always on the lookout for new and noteworthy finds, the team go out of their way to get their mitts on local distilleries' latest tipples – many of which are matched with seasonal ingredients in a thoroughly Instagrammable collection of cocktails.

Whether you grab a seat at the bar downstairs or head to the first floor for a quieter gin-sipping spot, rustic and comfortable decor creates a cosy atmosphere at Exeter's oldest cocktail joint.

ESTABLISHED
2006

GIN
30

SEATS
160

FOOD
Served

www.theoddfellowsbar.co.uk   01392 209050

35 Crocketts

2 Upper Paul Street, Exeter, Devon, EX4 3NB

Named after William Crockett who sold wines and spirits from Gandy Street in the 1840s, this is Exeter's only dedicated gin bar.

It specialises in artisan gins distilled across the South West - including Exeter, Salcombe, Curio and Tarquin's - and serves them from a dinky drinking den which rather deceptively stocks over 150 different sips.

'Book onto one of the regular gin talks or tastings'

An elegant handmade copper bar and a beautiful gin still (named Billy) complement the luxe decor which channels a gloriously grown-up vibe.

The team are hot on their spirits - ask for their latest fave pour or book yourself onto one of the regular gin talks or tastings and take your expertise to the next level.

ESTABLISHED
2017

GINS
150

SEATS
50

HOUSE GIN
Available

www.crockettsbar.co.uk   01392 332222

36 Rendezvous Wine Bar

38-40 Southernhay East, Exeter, Devon, EX1 1PE

When navigating Exeter's plethora of drinking holes serving cheap spirits and cocktails, one needs to be in the know to find the connoisseur's choice for wines, gins and spirits.

So head to leafy Southernhay and, down some hidden steps, you'll find this cosy basement bar which rewards with a wonderful selection of specialist sips.

Rendezvous' purist team avoid flavoured tonics and instead let the gin speak for itself. Take your pick from the 20-strong list (many South West-distilled) and enjoy gins at their best with a range of fine garnishes and tonics.

'Rewards with a selection of specialist sips'

With a daily-changing restaurant menu which focuses on local produce (and two beautiful gardens for summer drinking and dining), it's little wonder Rendezvous has gained numerous accolades since opening in 2006, including *Exeter Living*'s Best Restaurant 2017 and 2018.

ESTABLISHED
2006

GINS
20

SEATS
60

FOOD
Served

HOUSE GIN
Available

www.rendezvouswinebar.co.uk   01392 270222

37 Doctor Ink's Curiosities

Customs House, 43 The Quay, Exeter, Devon, EX2 4AN

The interior of this bijou and beautiful bar is much like one of its cocktails – complex and mysterious. Imagine a Victorian drinking den with a hint of bordello and a dash of luxe chic, hidden within a Grade I-listed building and you get the idea.

'The team scooped Imbibe's Best Themed Drinks List 2017'

Located on Exeter's quayside – a mere hop, skip and a jump from the city centre – this is one of the South West's most innovative cocktail bars. And its 80-strong collection of gins isn't too shabby either.

The endless drinks list includes the new Pride & Produce menu which showcases local and seasonal ingredients in creatively crafted concoctions. It's no wonder the team scooped *Imbibe's* Best Themed Drinks List 2017 and *Food Magazine's* Best Bar 2018.

ESTABLISHED
2016

GINS
80

SEATS
25

FOOD
Served

HOUSE GIN
Available

www.doctorinks.com   01392 491695

38 No. 3

3 Fore Street, Topsham, Devon, EX3 0HF

As a former pharmacy, this Topsham spot was once stocked with potions and pills; nowadays the prescription is premium gin.

A list of 38 juniper juices - which include a serious dose from the South West - are dispensed in a range of creative gin experiences, which often include herb garnishes grown in No. 3's secret garden.

The talented mixologists not only craft their own gins with some rather diverse botanicals, they're also up for helping gin fans develop their knowledge. Check out the regular Cocktail Making Masterclasses which will see you conquering three classic recipes.

'The talented mixologists craft their own gins with some rather diverse botanicals'

Too early for a Negroni? No. 3 also masquerades as a coffee house by day.

ESTABLISHED
2018

GINS
38

SEATS
60

FOOD
Served

HOUSE GIN
Available

www.no3topsham.co.uk   01392 877405

39 Spoken

43 The Strand, Exmouth, Devon, EX8 1AL

B it of a gin connoisseur? Tasted most of the current crop of artisan gins? However well-versed your palate is, we challenge you not to find something new behind the bar at Spoken.

Stocking 360 gins on a total spirits list of 1,200, it's little wonder this Exmouth find scooped the title of UK's Best Spirits Bar in the Great British Pub Awards 2017.

'UK's Best Spirits Bar in the Great British Pub Awards'

Despite the overwhelming number of options, don't swerve the opportunity to try the team's own-distilled spirit, Quick Gin, which is made nearby. Packed with ten botanicals including angelica root, nutmeg, liquorice and cinnamon, it's cracking with a slice of orange and also makes a knockout Negroni.

ESTABLISHED
2011

GINS
360

SEATS
45

FOOD
Served

HOUSE GIN
Available

www.spokenexmouth.com 01395 265228

40 The Headland Hotel

Daddyhole Road, Torquay, Devon, TQ1 2EF

Long, short, refreshing or sweet – whatever style of gin cocktail you prefer, at this elegant Torquay hotel it's always served with knockout views. An aperitif sipped in the sea air on the terrace is summertime bliss, while the Gallery Lounge makes a bright coastal hangout for imbibing craft creations and botanical concoctions (many distilled in the South West) from the 20-strong gin collection.

Pair gin with six courses served in the high-ceilinged, chandeliered Romanoff Restaurant (named after the Russian family who once owned this clifftop villa as their UK holiday home).

'An aperitif sipped in the sea air on the terrace is summertime bliss'

The house tipple is Start Point – botanicals distilled in yachty Salcombe taste exquisite against an ocean backdrop.

ESTABLISHED
1859

GINS
20

SEATS
100

FOOD
Served

HOUSE GIN
Available

www.headlandtorquay.com 01803 295666

41 Palace Hotel & Spa

Esplanade Road, Paignton, Devon, TQ4 6BJ

The Palace Hotel was originally built as the home of Washington Singer, son of the founder of the Singer Sewing Machine Company.

Now a classic hotel on the English Riviera, it's a great spot in which to relive the gin-sipping glamour of a bygone age.

Head to the Washington Bar or settle in a raffia chair in The Singer Lounge and peruse a gin menu which includes South West spirits such as Conker, Trevethan, Tarquin's and Salcombe gins. There are no cocktails here: it's all about the classic G&T.

'A great spot in which to relive the gin-sipping glamour of a bygone age'

After your aperitif, head in to supper at The Paris Restaurant. Looking for a daytime visit? Plump for a traditional afternoon tea and make it boozy with a gin accompaniment.

ESTABLISHED
2001

GINS
11

SEATS
26

FOOD
Served

HOUSE GIN
Available

www.palacepaignton.com 01803 555121

42 Soar Mill Cove Hotel

Soar Mill Cove, Malborough, Salcombe, Devon, TQ7 3DS

A haunt of the late, great Audrey Hepburn, Soar Mill Cove has been a destination for the in-crowd exploring the charms of nearby Salcombe for some 40 years. Its stunning sea views are reason alone to schedule a visit.

Guests' fave aperitif is Jen's Gin Fizz, which is made with the house gin, a splash of homemade elderflower cordial and a dash of Taittinger champagne. The botanicals in the gin are hand picked from the valley and include gorse blossom, samphire, and honey made by the family.

'Botanicals are hand picked from the valley and include gorse blossom and samphire'

In addition to exploring the gin list at the bar, keep an eye open for occasional gin dinners which include fizz on arrival, a gin tasting and a beautiful three course supper, followed by a Q&A with a distiller.

ESTABLISHED
1978

GINS
10

SEATS
40

FOOD
Served

HOUSE GIN
Available

www.soarmillcove.co.uk   01548 561566

DARTINGTON

CRYSTAL

PROUD SPONSOR
OF THE

INDEPENDENT
GIN
GUIDE

DARTINGTON.CO.UK

43 Boringdon Hall Hotel & Spa

Colebrook, Plympton, Plymouth, Devon, PL7 4DP

With a name that comes from the Saxon term for 'enchanted place on the hill', this is a rather magnificent setting for any gin experience.

Whether you choose a classic gin and tonic by the roaring fire in the Great Hall or a quirky gin cocktail in The Secret Bar, all of the drinks are crafted to thrill the senses.

'Build and control the intensity of flavours using the likes of cubeb berries and dried rose petals'

There's also a bespoke element to the experience: the bartenders encourage visitors to choose the garnish for their gin so, for example, you can build and control the intensity of flavours through the likes of cubeb berries and dried rose petals.

This creative approach makes complete sense in a setting that's also home to Scott Paton's three AA rosette Gallery Restaurant with its exquisitely crafted dishes.

ESTABLISHED
2011

GINS
15

SEATS
40

FOOD
Served

HOUSE GIN
Available

www.boringdonhall.co.uk   01752 344455

44 Barbican Botanics Gin Room

38 New Street, Plymouth, Devon, PL1 2NA

Tucked away along a cobbled street on Plymouth's historic Barbican, this charming little gin shop and tasting room is a must-visit.

Housed in a 15th century, Grade II-listed merchant's house, Barbican Botanics Gin Room embodies Britain's long obsession with this curious spirit.

'Housed in a 15th century, Grade II listed merchant's house'

With a healthy collection of more than a hundred gins, this is a find for a pre-dinner aperitif or even an after-work drink, but be prepared to make it a regular haunt if you're planning to make your way through the entire list.

One not to miss is the house Barbican Botanics Gin – a fresh and earthy spirit which draws on milk thistle and fennel seed botanicals.

ESTABLISHED
2018

GINS
100

SEATS
30

FOOD
Served

HOUSE GIN
Available

www.littleginbox.com

45 The Arundell Arms

Fore Street, Lifton, Devon, PL16 0AA

Straddling the Devon and Cornwall border, this family-run hotel, restaurant and bar prides itself on the provenance of its food sourcing – which also extends to the growing gin collection.

Thanks to the hotel's location, the spirit shelf features crowning jewels from both county's gin scenes. If you're up for a G&T, take your pick from 12 craft distillers, or go a little more off-piste and explore the well-considered gin cocktail list which includes specific details of each glass and garnish used.

'Go off piste and explore the well considered gin cocktail list'

From horse riding and clay pigeon shooting to trout fishing, this is a spot for indulging in quintessentially British pursuits – which, of course, includes imbibing gin.

ESTABLISHED
1935

GINS
12

SEATS
110

FOOD
Served

HOUSE GIN
Available

46 Blue Plate Restaurant

Main Road, Downderry, Torpoint, Cornwall, PL11 3LD

This south coast coffee shop, restaurant, deli and bar is a rare find as it's somewhere to shop for gifts, sip a cocktail, eat dinner and stock up on local gins, all in one visit.

'Fowey Gin served with pink grapefruit tonic and garnished with caramelised grapefruit'

Twenty-three gins feature – each served in a bespoke style to best set off its specific botanicals – and prove to be a pukka pairing with fresh local fish, River Fowey mussels, lobster and pasture-reared meats. And make sure you order a side of freshly baked sourdough to accompany your piscatorial pleasures.

On the local gin front, Fowey Gin (with pink grapefruit tonic and garnished with caramelised grapefruit) or Trevethan Gin (made just ten miles away) are the sips of choice. And if you're a keen gin fan, keep an eye open for gin and dinner events and meet-the-distiller tastings.

ESTABLISHED
2010

GINS
23

SEATS
68

FOOD
Served

www.blueplatecornwall.co.uk   01503 250308

17 Old Quay House Hotel

28 Fore Street, Fowey, Cornwall, PL23 1AQ

Take a seat on the Old Quay House's waterside terrace and sip a crisp gin and tonic while watching boats bobbing in the Fowey estuary.

As befitting such a maritime location, Salcombe Gin's yachty Start Point is the house pour – the Salcombe team even run a pop-up gin bar here occasionally.

"There are plenty of options to keep you going until dinner, including the classic Gin Martini"

However, the gin list is 17-strong, so there are plenty of options to keep you going until dinner, including the classic Gin Martini which the team serve with style.

Do stick around to dine as the restaurant is top notch (plump for local mussels in season). Then finish the evening with a nightcap on the terrace as the sun dips below the horizon.

ESTABLISHED
2004

GINS
17

SEATS
30

FOOD
Served

HOUSE GIN
Available

www.theoldquayhouse.com   01726 833302

48 Carlyon Bay Hotel

Sea Road, St Austell, Cornwall, PL25 3RD

Perched on a clifftop above Cornwall's sparkling coastline and with splendid views over St Austell Bay, this smart hotel is a definite contender for 'G&T with the best view'. Take your pick from the 20 gins behind the bar and head out onto the spacious terrace with your new fave find.

The spirit offering has a strong focus on provenance with many of the bottles sourced from local distilleries, including a full range of gins and pastis from Cornwall's Tarquin's.

'A definite contender for "G&T with the best view"'

In winter, cosy up in the comfortable lounge with a cocktail aperitif before heading through for an evening of feasting on local fare in the art deco-style dining room.

ESTABLISHED
1932

GINS
20

SEATS
150

FOOD
Served

HOUSE GIN
Available

49 The Pickwick Inn

Burgois, St Issey, Padstow, Cornwall, PL27 7QQ

This family-run inn takes a little navigating to find, but you don't get breathtaking estuary views and the title of north Cornwall's hidden gem if you're slap bang on the busy Atlantic Highway. Some things are worth the effort.

'Kick off with a Cornish Garden cocktail and a plate of briny Porthilly oysters'

Intrepid travellers are rewarded with a stonking drinks list - and great food to match - which champions Cornish greats like Tarquin's alongside local micro distilleries such as Rock Gin.

Not sure where to start your gin journey? Grab a table by the window and kick off with a Cornish Garden cocktail (Rock Gin, elderflower cordial, Cornish apple juice, lime, thyme and cucumber ribbon) and a plate of briny Porthilly oysters plucked from the beds in the estuary below - and the rest will follow.

ESTABLISHED
1981

GINS
17

SEATS
160

FOOD
Served

www.pickwickinn.co.uk   01841 540361

50 Ruby's Bar

18 Broad Street, Padstow, Cornwall, PL28 8EA

Tucked away a short distance from Padstow's busy harbour, this unassuming but rather special find also happens to be a member of Rick and Jill Stein's foodie family.

Secure a seat at the candle-lit – and usually chocka – bar and journey your way through a list of 30 gins that hail all the way from Auckland to nearby Wadebridge.

'Rick's Ceylon Negroni is a house favourite'

Award-winning bartender, Mr Lyan, has created a cocktail for each member of the Stein clan and Rick's Ceylon Negroni is a favourite with the punters.

With chic interiors suggesting its coastal location, this is your go-to for a leisurely nightcap after dinner at The Seafood Restaurant.

ESTABLISHED
2016

GINS
30

SEATS
25

HOUSE GIN
Available

51 Fistral Beach Hotel and Spa

Esplanade Road, Newquay, Cornwall, TR7 1PT

If local gin with a dash of peeling waves and briny air features high on your hit list, Fistral Beach Hotel in north Cornwall is a must visit.

Overlooking its (world famous) namesake beach, the coastal-chic hotel harbours panoramic views of the ocean. Kick back on the deck – or head inside to the comfort of the contemporary Bay Bar – and, with an expertly crafted drink in hand, watch the surfers carve through the breakers.

"With an expertly crafted drink in hand, watch the surfers carve through the breakers"

The house serve features the bar's own Fistral Gin, which is packed with notes of pink grapefruit, fennel, pink peppercorn, elderflower and orange peel. It's the perfect reward after a bracing walk on the beach.

ESTABLISHED
2013

GINS
10

SEATS
200

FOOD
Served

HOUSE GIN
Available

www.fistralbeachhotel.co.uk   01637 852221

52 The Old Grammar School

19 St Mary's Street, Truro, Cornwall, TR1 2AF

A long-time fave on the Truro cocktail scene, this is your go-to for an 18-strong gin list which includes a cracking core from Cornish distillers.

The gins are supplied by North Coast Wines who come up trumps with a regularly-changing collection of curious and unusual finds which includes the likes of Westward Farm Gin from the Isles of Scilly.

'It's the signature cocktail list where things get beautifully creative'

Each gin is elegantly served to show off its unique flavours via a specific garnish and tonic, but it's the signature cocktail list where things get beautifully creative. Especially good is the Cornish Bramble: Elemental Cornish Gin and Elemental Raspberry Cornish Gin with a little sugar and lemon, shaken over ice and garnished with raspberries and edible flowers.

ESTABLISHED
2010

GINS
18

SEATS
60

FOOD
Served

HOUSE GIN
Available

www.theoldgrammarschool.com   01872 278559

53 The Rosevine

Near Portscatho, Truro, Cornwall, TR2 5EW

This family-friendly foodie hotel is also a find for gin lovers. You don't need to compromise on the perfect pour just because your partner wants top-notch dining or the kids demand you stay no more than a stone's throw from the beach, as The Rosevine does it all.

So choose your moment and head to the cosy lounge or leafy garden, where you can savour your pick of the gins along with views of the Cornish coastline.

Locally distilled Fowey Valley, Tarquin's or Trevethan Honey Oak Cornish Gin make for an elegant G&T, or plump for a classic Bramble served with a double shot of Tarquin's, sugar syrup, fresh lemon juice and crème de mure.

'Pair your visit with a gin tasting evening'

And if you just happen to pair your visit with one of the gin tasting evenings, it's pure coincidence. Right?

ESTABLISHED
2001

GINS
10

SEATS
30

FOOD
Served

www.rosevine.co.uk   01872 580206

54 Dolly's Tea Room

21 Church Street, Falmouth, Cornwall, TR11 3EG

There aren't many places where you can flick through *Vanity Fair*, sip a copa glass of G&T and indulge in a slice of homemade victoria sponge while listening to the tinkly strains of live piano, but hey, there aren't many places like Dolly's.

'Try the Falmouth famous Vicar's Tea Party or the Flapper's Delight'

This gin palace is a gloriously eccentric and elaborate experience where you'll encounter an incredible list of over 300 gins within its Georgian walls.

A real life Mad Hatter's tea party, cocktails are served in quirky mismatched china teapots and teacups in all shapes and sizes.

Try the Falmouth-famous Vicar's Tea Party and the Flapper's Delight, or indulge in a pleasingly boozy afternoon tea served with gin jam.

ESTABLISHED
2011

GINS
300

SEATS
40

FOOD
Served

www.dollysbar.co.uk   01326 218400

55 The Bay Hotel

Coverack, Helston, Cornwall, TR12 6TF

This oceanside hotel bar with its cool coastal palette stocks a decent line in premium gins – 30 to be precise. What's much more unusual, however, is that 18 of these are distilled in Cornwall.

From shore to moor, every element of the Cornish landscape is represented via the botanicals waiting to be discovered. And the team serve each pour with equal attention to detail.

'Pair your gin with juicy lobster which is hauled in fresh from the bay'

If you want to experience a food and gin-paired taste of Cornwall, match your gin with juicy lobster which is hauled in fresh from the bay, and dine while drinking in the awesome seascape view.

ESTABLISHED
2006

GINS
30

SEATS
40

FOOD
Served

HOUSE GIN
Available

www.thebayhotel.co.uk   01326 280464

56 Halsetown Inn

Halsetown, St Ives, Cornwall, TR26 3NA

S ituated a stone's throw from the seaside town of St Ives, this cosy pub oozes rustic charm and character.

Halsetown's extensive gin list has the power to lure any water-lover to shore, and features interesting finds from small batch St Ives Gin to Japanese craft gin, Roku.

In addition to 40 G&T opportunities, the inn stumps up a bill of cocktails which includes Southside Fizz – a blast of St Ives Gin, lemon juice, syrup and soda finished with mint from the garden.

'Interesting finds, from small batch St Ives Gin to Japanese craft gin, Roku'

The local ethos extends to the kitchen too, where a brilliant band of chefs fashion a fabulous menu of Cornish fare. Tip: the Sunday roast is a must.

ESTABLISHED
2016

GINS
40

SEATS
70

FOOD
Served

HOUSE GIN
Available

GIN STORES

Where to stock your drinks cabinet with unusual and specialist gins

57 Great Western Wine

Unit 3-4 Wells Road, Bath, BA2 3AP

Southwest oenophiles congregate at Great Western for its award winning portfolio of fine wines (it scooped IWC South West Merchant of the Year four years in a row), but this quality Bath boutique also keeps a spirited secret in its cellars: a stonking selection of exotic gins.

ESTABLISHED
1983

GINS
150

'This quality Bath boutique also keeps a spirited secret in its cellars'

In addition to showcasing top quality regional gins such as Salcombe, Conker and Tarquin's, you'll also find a selection of more unusual international picks, including French Audemus with its Spanish pink peppercorns.

Check the website for details of regular gin events and creative cocktail recipes.

www.greatwesternwine.co.uk   01225 322810

58 Johns of Instow & Appledore

4–5 Marine Parade, Instow, Devon, EX39 4HY

'Try before you buy' is the motto at this multi-award winning north Devon delicatessen and drinks emporium. Though sampling the whole spectrum of 18 speciality gins on one trip would be a stretch for even the most seasoned spirit connoisseur.

ESTABLISHED
1926

GINS
18

'Cocktail classes and meet-the-producer events showcase local distilleries'

The family-run deli and cafe has supplied the people of north Devon with quality homemade and local produce since 1926, and visitors still queue out of the doors of its Instow and Appledore venues for the outstanding range of artisan spirits, cheeses, charcuterie and fresh bakery products.

Cocktail classes and meet-the-producer events showcase the local distilleries represented on Johns' shelves and you can even sip a G&T with lunch at the cafe before picking up bottles to-go.

www.johnsofinstow.co.uk   01271 860310

59 Regency Wines

20-22 Apple Lane, Sowton Industrial Estate, Exeter, Devon, EX2 5GL

Over half of the gins stocked on Regency's shelves are crafted in the South West - an astonishing amount in a full collection that exceeds 150 different bottles.

As specialist wholesalers to the licensed trade, the clued-up team train bartenders to create the perfect serve, as well as host courses and masterclasses for the gin-loving public at venues across the region.

'Hosting gin courses and masterclasses for the gin-loving public'

If you're visiting the shop on the outskirts of Exeter, don't leave without also browsing the extensive wine collection - there are some gems from Slovenia, Bulgaria and Greece among the impressive selection. The Cornish Morvenna Rum is also a worthy drinks cabinet contender.

ESTABLISHED
2001

GINS
150

www.regencywines.co.uk   01392 444123

60 Darts Farm

Topsham, near Exeter, Devon, EX3 0QH

The craftsmanship, quality and passion of the region's top gin geniuses are bottled in Darts' 50-strong curation of juniper juice. And each distillery included demonstrates the expertise required to create a world-class gin.

Sip a Salcombe Gin and Luscombe Light Devon Tonic in the restaurant, meet distillers at taster events or book a masterclass evening with Susy Atkins: a chance to sample a superb selection of gins, learn how they're crafted and experiment with garnishes.

'Sip a Salcombe Gin and Luscombe Light Devon Tonic in the restaurant'

Topsham's nationally award-winning lifestyle destination (still with a working farm at its heart) not only stocks a corking collection of spirits, it also features a huge range of bottled beers, ciders and wines, and has experts on hand to help visitors choose a new favourite tipple.

ESTABLISHED
1971

GINS
50

www.dartsfarm.co.uk   01392 878200

61 The Tipsy Merchant

13 High Street, Budleigh Salterton, Devon, EX9 6LD

Spirit sippers are usually tempted into The Tipsy Merchant by the creative window displays. But once inside, they're thoroughly seduced by the tastings, the opportunity to book gin evenings and the delights of restocking their home collection with bottles from the region's finest distillers.

The Budleigh Salterton store hosts a number of gin evenings each year, and the samples, nibbles and tasty discounts at each one mean that swift booking is essential to secure a spot. If you're not lucky this time, try a Tipsy sampling afternoon featuring local distilleries instead.

'Samples, nibbles and tasty discounts at each one means that swift booking is essential'

Oenophile? Follow the juniper jollities by perusing the collection of over 300 wines and cracking selection of local beers and ciders.

ESTABLISHED
2017

GINS
100

www.thetipsymerchant.co.uk   01395 443943

62 Wildmoor Fine Food & Drink

43 Fore Street, Bovey Tracey, Devon, TQ13 9AD

Bovey Tracey's Wildmoor ensures all gin lovers exploring Dartmoor can take home a bounty of spirits from the South West and further afield.

The team's passion for promoting appreciation of quality gin is apparent in everything from the mini tastings in store to the serving of Negronis in the cafe and courtyard.

'Gin lovers exploring Dartmoor can take home a bounty of spirits'

Managing partner Jeremy Clevett launched the Westcountry Gin Masterclass in 2018 to educate juniper fans and develop their tasting and pairing skills. And after a sellout event at Dartmoor Whisky Distillery it's now hit the road, partnering with venues to champion the region's most distinguished spirits.

ESTABLISHED
2015

GINS
25

SALCOMBE
GIN®

PROUD SPONSOR
OF THE

INDEPENDENT
GIN
GUIDE

SALCOMBEGIN.COM

63 Barbican Botanics Gin Room

38 New Street, Plymouth, Devon, PL1 2NA

Spirit connoisseurs will already be familiar with Little Gin Box, the artfully curated gin subscription service from Barbican Botanics. And this year the gin-sperts behind the nifty initiative have launched their first bricks-and-mortar shop.

ESTABLISHED
2018

GINS
100

'The gin-sperts behind the nifty initiative have launched their first bricks-and-mortar shop'

Set in one of Plymouth's original 15th century merchant's houses, the boutique store stocks over a hundred UK gins. There's a strong focus on provenance, small batch spirits and indie distilleries. Quaff your drink at the bar or pick between the comfy lounge and enclosed garden sipping spots.

Along with meet-the-maker evenings, the team also host tastings and events.

64 North Coast Wine Company

1 Lansdown Road, Bude, Cornwall, EX23 8BH

There's a treasure trove of artisan spirits and interesting fine wines to be discovered at this indie bottle shop and bar.

A short detour off the A39, this is the perfect pit-stop to pick up a few tipsy tokens of your jollies on the rugged north Cornwall coast. Passengers can relax and enjoy the crop of Cornish gins at the in-house bar, while designated drivers imbibe an expertly-roasted coffee.

'Explore the rum offering which features 40 bottles from around the world'

The knowledgeable team are always happy to help visitors choose from the collection of 25 gins, 600 bins, 300 spirits and rotating roster of local craft beers and ciders. And if you've reached peak gin on your travels, explore the rum offering which features 40 bottles from around the world.

ESTABLISHED
2009

GINS
25

www.ncwine.co.uk   01288 354304

65 Ellis Wharton Wines

St Andrews Road, Par, Cornwall, PL24 2LX

It may be diminutive in size, but EWW delivers big time on its unique curation of international wines and spirits – many organic and biodynamic.

On the juniper front, Cornish distillers create the core of the collection, although browsers will also find a smart selection from the wider South West – and beyond. In keeping with their support of the region, the team have also launched a gin with Wrecking Coast to raise funds for Cornwall Air Ambulance.

'A unique curation of international wines and spirits – many organic and biodynamic'

There are usually a few choice bottles open for sampling, so curious sippers can explore a little before deciding which one to take home for further "research".

ESTABLISHED
2006

GINS
70

GIN
SCHOOLS

Develop your gin tasting and distilling skills

66 Devon Distillery

The Shops at Dartington, Shinners Bridge, Dartington, Devon, TQ9 6TQ

This is the (stationary) sister to Devon Distillery's popular 'Still on the Move' mobile gin experience.

Visit to spend a fun and productive session learning the art of gin distillation at this delightful micro distillery which is tucked away at The Shops at Dartington.

Choose botanicals to please your palate, do some hands-on distilling, then bottle and brand your unique and personalised gin.

'Upgrade to a 70cl bottle as it's rather special to be able to serve your own creation'

We'd recommend upgrading to a 70cl bottle as it's rather special to be able to serve your own creation next time you have chums over for drinks.

ESTABLISHED
2018

MAXIMUM GROUP
8

PRICES FROM
£65

www.devonginschool.co.uk   01803 812509

67 Salcombe Gin School

The Boathouse, 28-30 Island Street, Salcombe, Devon, TQ8 8DP

There have always been a number of good reasons to mosey down to Salcombe with its lapping turquoise waters and millionaires' pads, but since 2016 gin has been top of the list.

It all changed with the launch of Salcombe Distilling Co. and now enthusiasts flock to learn how to craft their own gin at the distillery. Under the guidance of the experts, distil 70cl of unique spirit in a beautiful bottle with bespoke label (mulling over the name is all part of the fun).

'Unleash your creativity on a bounty of botanicals and a mini copper still'

The half-day sessions kick off with a talk through the distilling process and a peek at how it's done on a grand scale, before you get to unleash your creativity on a bounty of botanicals and a mini copper still.

ESTABLISHED
2016

MAXIMUM GROUP
16

PRICES FROM
£100

www.salcombegin.com   01548 288180

The Pickwick Inn
No. 49

68 Experiences An Mor

An Mor Hotel, Hartland Terrace, Bude, Cornwall, EX23 8JY

The quirky and quintessentially British An Mor Hotel in Bude harbours a rather enticing secret: it's home to a beautiful copper-suffused gin school.

Visitors to its gin masterclasses not only get to learn all about the history of the spirit and taste different gin flavours, they also get to create their own bespoke recipe.

Pick from an alluring range of botanicals and, using a copper still, distil 50cl of unique spirit which you'll label to take home.

'Pick from an alluring range of botanicals and distil 50cl of unique gin'

Each class finishes with the participants enjoying a glass of the gin they've carefully crafted. Also available are two-hour gin parties (which include hands-on distilling), hour-long gin tastings on Fridays and Saturdays, and gin-inspired high teas.

ESTABLISHED
2017

MAXIMUM GROUP
8

PRICES FROM
£25

www.experiencesanmor.co.uk   01288 355460

MORE GOOD
GIN
HAUNTS

Additional finds for your little black book

69
BEER & BIRD

18a Fore Street, St Ives,
Cornwall, TR26 1AB

www.beerandbird.com

70
THE BREAK

Beach House, Marine Drive,
Widemouth Bay, Bude,
Cornwall, EX23 0AW

www.beachhousewidemouth.co.uk

71
BUSTOPHER JONES

62 Lemon Street, Truro,
Cornwall, TR1 2PN

www.bustopher-jones.co.uk

72
COPPER BAR

Penventon Park Hotel, West End,
Redruth, Cornwall, TR15 1TE

www.penventon.co.uk

73
COX & BALONEY
TEAROOM AND BAR

182 & 184 Cheltenham Road,
Bristol, BS6 5RB

www.coxandbaloneytearooms.com

74
THE DARK HORSE

7a Kingsmead Square, Bath, BA1 2AB

www.darkhorsebar.co.uk

75
THE EASTBURY HOTEL

Long Street, Sherborne,
Dorset, DT9 3BY

www.theeastburyhotel.co.uk

76
THE GREENBANK HOTEL

Harbourside, Falmouth,
Cornwall, TR11 2SR

www.greenbank-hotel.co.uk

77
THE IDLE ROCKS

Harbourside, St Mawes,
Cornwall, TR2 5AN

www.idlerocks.com

78
THE KENSINGTON ARMS

35-37 Stanley Road, Redland,
Bristol, BS6 6NP

www.thekensingtonarms.co.uk

79
MULLION COVE HOTEL

Mullion, Helston,
Cornwall, TR12 7EP

www.mullion-cove.co.uk

80
NO.13 GIN & COCKTAIL BAR

13 Montpellier Street, Montpellier,
Cheltenham, GL50 1SU

www.johngordons.co.uk

81
THE PUMP HOUSE

Merchants Road, Hotwells,
Bristol, BS8 4PZ

www.the-pumphouse.com

82
THE QUEENS ARMS

Corton Denham, Sherborne,
Somerset, DT9 4LR

www.thequeensarms.com

83
THE REDAN INN

Fry's Well, Chilcompton, Radstock,
Somerset, BA3 4HA

www.theredaninn.co.uk

84
THE RUMMER

All Saints Lane, Bristol, BS1 1JH

www.therummer.net

85
SALCOMBE HARBOUR HOTEL

Cliff Road, Salcombe, Devon, TQ8 8JH

www.harbourhotels.co.uk

86
THE SWAN

Station Road, Bampton,
Devon, EX16 9NG

www.theswan.co

GIN STORES

Additional finds for your little black book

87
THE BOTTLE BANK

2 Tidemill House, Discovery Quay,
Falmouth, Cornwall, TR11 3XP

www.thebottlebank.co.uk

88
CHRISTOPHER PIPER WINES

1 Silver Street, Ottery St Mary,
Devon, EX11 1DB

www.christopherpiperwines.co.uk

89
CORKS OF COTHAM

54 Cotham Hill, Bristol, BS6 6JX

www.corksofbristol.com

90
DARTMOUTH WINE COMPANY

6 Duke Street, Dartmouth,
Devon, TQ6 9PZ

91
GRAPE & GRIND

101 Gloucester Road, Bristol, BS7 8AT

www.grapeandgrind.co.uk

92
INDEPENDENT SPIRIT OF BATH

7 Terrace Walk, Bath, BA1 1LN

www.independentspiritofbath.co.uk

93
JOHN GORDONS

11 Montpellier Arcade, Montpellier,
Cheltenham, GL50 1SU

www.johngordons.co.uk

94
JOHNS THE LIQUOR CELLAR

75 Fore Street, St Ives,
Cornwall, TR26 1HW

www.theliquorcellar.co.uk

95
MAWGAN STORES

Higher Lane, Mawgan,
Cornwall, TR12 6AT

www.mawganstores.co.uk

96
PADSTOW FARM SHOP

Trethillick Farm, Padstow,
Cornwall, PL28 8HJ

www.padstowfarmshop.co.uk

97
THE SHOPS AT DARTINGTON

Shinners Bridge, Dartington, Totnes,
Devon, TQ9 6TQ

www.dartington.org

98
TOTNES WINE COMPANY

36 High Street, Totnes,
Devon, TQ9 5RY

www.totneswine.com

99
WADEBRIDGE WINES

Eddystone Road, Wadebridge,
Cornwall, PL27 7AL

www.wadebridgewines.co.uk

100
WEBER AND TRING'S

14 Christmas Steps, Bristol, BS1 5BS

www.weberandtrings.co.uk

MEET OUR
Committee

The *Independent Gin Guide* committee has worked closely with the South West gin community and the team at Salt Media in the creation of this year's guide

Susy Atkins

Consultant editor

Award winning drinks writer, presenter and author, Susy writes the weekly wine column for the *Sunday Telegraph*'s *Stella* magazine and is drinks editor for *delicious.* magazine and *Food Magazine.* She also co-hosts *The Telegraph* Gin Experience each summer.

Susy enjoyed a 12-year stint as one of the regular wine experts on BBC1's flagship cookery show, *Saturday Kitchen,* and appears regularly with celebrity chefs presenting wines at food festivals and events in the UK and abroad. She is the author and/or editor of 11 books on drink and wine and has won several awards including a *Food & Travel Magazine* Readers' Award for Best Drinks Book.

Friday night tipple?
'A fine local gin with a light premium tonic (not too much), and two large ice cubes, garnished with a twisted slice of lime. Simple, clean, classic.'

Nick Cooper

Publisher

Publisher at Salt Media, Nick is the co-founder of *Food Magazine* and the award winning *Insider's Guide* series (which includes the *Trencherman's Guide* and *Indy Coffee Guides* for the South West and South Wales, North of England and North Wales, Scotland, and Ireland).

He's spent the last 15 years eating and drinking his way around the South West and beyond.

Friday night tipple?
'A good Negroni served in a chunky cut-glass tumbler gets any weekend off to a swinging start.'

Abby Millar

Contributing writer and drinks consultant

Food and drink marketing specialist (and partner in Altum Media), Abby works with both small artisan producers and national brands.

She successfully crowdfunded Dartmoor Whisky Distillery and helped launch the Cooper King Distillery Founders' Club. Abby regularly works with Dartmoor Whisky Distillery, Quicke's, Little's Coffee and Roastworks Coffee Roasters and has her finger on the pulse of the buzzing South West food and drink scene.

Friday night tipple?
'A classic British gin Bramble served in a chilled and heavy old fashioned glass.'

INDEX